Living

with

Divine Intervention

Inspirational Poetry
for the Heart, Mind and Soul

B. Chuck Thomas
"TheOldPoetHimself"

3G Publishing, Inc.
Loganville, Ga 30052
www.3gpublishinginc.com
Phone: 1-888-442-9637

First published by 3G Publishing, Inc. July, 2021

ISBN: 9781941247921

Printed in the United States of America

Acknowledgements

Thank you to my family and friends for the continued support and inspirational words. Thank you to all of those who have opened their hearts and minds to the poetry. Thank you to my wife and daughter for the consistent walk with me and the Lord.

Thank you most of all Jesus Christ for the words and phrases.

Introduction

The poems following were inspired through actual experiences, meditation and personal reflection. Some of the poems are filled with emotion that resulted from personal friends' and relatives' trials and struggles. Some poems reflect the social climate and spiritual departure. Some poems offer a different insight on praise and worship. Some of the poetry strikes to the soul of the Christian as we attempt to fully live the Word. The divine intervention is evident with the strong spiritual references. As you read the poetry, I am confident that you will be internally blessed and forever changed. Enjoy!

The Call

Awaken in your walk for a new beginning in the Spirit!

B. Chuck Thomas
"TheOldPoetHimself"

Table of Contents

<u>Accounting</u>

As you awaken from your slumber
And arise from your sleep
Good intentions crowd your spirit
But still the evil seems to seep

A prayer to start on good things
A concentration to keep great thought
With a view of salvation ever growing
Knowing your soul's already bought

The sin still seems to hover 'round you
And your sins just seem to mount
Don't let the evil fill you over
With God just keep a short account

Stop the evil in its path
Call out all sin throughout the day
Pray now for God to pull you over
Then turn from sin, the other way

Your sinful listing, keep it small
Ask for forgiveness right away
Let your account remain with Jesus
And in God's Grace you will still stay

Mark 11:25

And when ye stand praying, forgive, if ye have ought against any: that your Father also which is in heaven may forgive you your trespasses.

Blessed Me

Sometimes I wonder why God blessed me
Over all the other men in the world
I wonder why He touched me so
And gave me a special little girl

Sometimes I wonder why God blessed me
More than any other man in life
To give me a beautiful flower
Dedicated to being a mother and good wife

Oh God You stayed with me and showed me how
Your favor can grow so great
I should have thanked You years ago
I thank You now…it's not too late

As I wonder in my thoughts Lord
And I pause to glance on You
No I can't see You but I feel You
I cherish the blessing that You do

I wonder on my life's journey
From a boy now to a man
Realizing how life is granted Lord
As my will is in Your Hand

Blessed Father…Thank You Lord
For all the blessings that I feel and see
For Lord I cherish the special family
That You lovingly blessed on me

Colossians 3:24

Knowing that of the Lord ye shall receive the reward of the inheritance: for ye serve the Lord Christ.

<u>Casket Thought</u>

And now the time to cut has come
And there no longer be
For you must know you're truly worth
More than just minutes three!

Who'll lead the cause to speak my end
To sum up all my life!
Who'll lead the cause to speak the words
Of sons, daughters and wife!

Don't hold me to some seconds
For you have some things to do
But give all my mourners refuge
To see their sadness through

A lifelong friend or newly meet
The touch of lives are true
"Now sum it in three minutes" or
All eyes will be on you

*If there is somewhere you need to be
Then GO!......I have all Day
But don't stop the tribute to my life
And things my loved ones say!*

And think of you when your time comes
Your life with things to sum
How would you feel, If you could feel
For three minutes and you're done

Christian World

Funny, it is all about business
When it all goes against me
But quickly turns to friendship and Jesus
When the advantage is for you I see.

Oh yeah, we have to understand their spirit
You know...we all have some room to grow
Seem that's an excuse to excuse selfishness
Just deal with childish stuff more and more

Hey they're all still your Christian brothers
Be strong and turn the other cheek
I know that forgiveness is essential
The main element of the God for Whom I seek

Don't worry about all the words you hear
Don't worry about the things they say
Persecution comes as part of being a servant
Just learn to get by everyday

I'll keep letting You guide my steps
I'll trust in Your Will I'll understand
I'll work to keep my walk with You
And become a better Christian man

John 15:19

If ye were of the world, the world would love his own: but because ye are not of the world, but I have chosen you out of the world, therefore the world hateth you.

<u>Confidence</u>

But Thou O Lord are a shield for me
Stopping circumstances negative that I cannot see
Causing me to take heed to the scripture that's read
My glory and lifter up of my head

Studying to understand and then sin to flee
For Thou O Lord are a shield for me
Re-evaluating the sermon and what the preacher said
The Glory and lifter up of my head

I praise you Lord and thank you from my knees
For Thou O Lord are a shield for me
I will focus my heart and be Spirit lead
You are my glory and lifter up of my head

I must stand strong Lord that is my decree
For Thou O Lord are a shield for me
Fighting this battle till my soul is put to bed
My glory and lifter up of my head

Be bold, look up look up to see
For Thou O Lord are a shield for me
It is You that I trust and by Your Words I'm fed
You are The Glory and lifter up of my head

Psalm 3:3

But thou, O LORD, art a shield for me; my glory, and the lifter up of mine head.

<u>Expectation</u>

The thunder will rumble
A flash of light
The wind will be moving
Expect the rain

The darkness continues
The moon seems half full
The star has less twinkle
Expect the morning light

The seed is now entered
The ground is made great
The water and the sunlight
Expect the plant

I do what I want
And I talk as I please
I think about things
Just don't touch on my knees

Expect the death.......Hell

Proverbs 11:7

When a wicked man dieth, his expectation shall perish: and the hope of unjust men perisheth.

Explanation

God you did it!
God you did it!
God you did it again!
I don't know how

God you did it!
God you did it!
I don't know how
But I'm so happy now

God you did it!
God you did it so fresh
God you did it so new
God you did it!
God you loved me too

God you did it!
God you did it!
God you did it!
Thank you God
Bless Your Name

God You did it!
And through Jesus Christ
I pray!

Proverbs 3:5-6

Trust in the LORD with all thine heart; and lean not unto thine own understanding. In all thy ways acknowledge him, and he shall direct thy paths.

Facilitation-No Broken Pen

I did not stop the words from God
I still write them down in a book
I tried to share them with His People
But seems the words were mistook

When I stand for things of Jesus
And His Truth is the same
My righteous brothers pull against me
And some scandalize on my name

It is a shame for those who claim Christ
To sit and side with the world
To side with Jesus there is a straight line
Not a dip and a curve

It is preached as Christians, we are in the world
But don't walk in this land
But when you are pressed for Christ
Like Peter, some seem to side with just man

There is a price to pay for choosing
I'll stick with God in my route
Because when you stay stuck in the middle
God says He'll spew you right out

Revelation 3:16

So then because thou art lukewarm, and neither cold nor hot, I will spue thee out of my mouth.

<u>Front Row</u>

A time is always coming
It is coming 'till it comes
It has happened to every other
It touches all...not just some

Get some scripture in your bosom
Gaining Jesus is a start
When that time will come for you
You can use what's in your heart

The time and moments just seem to pause
One day just stalls as time stands still
All kinds of emotions take you over
And you can't voice out how you feel

Pray now to God for He must know
Lean on His Word to help you so
The time has come you lost a glow
It is your time on the front row

<u>Good Looking</u>

Alignment with a pretty face
Standing with winners of a race
And be with those of seemingly health
And give a big ear with those of wealth

When the Christian walk is spirited
And the Spirit seeks its kind
But focus is on flesh
Magnifying the struggles to find

Or so we easily like to cling
Or somehow gather and just mesh
With the successful of life
And the greatness of flesh

Nothing is wrong with the silver
Or the gold that is gained
But letting those two be the standard
Leaves the soul on a plain

That open wilderness field
With no direction that seems clear
Gives all credentials to sin
Then to God is no fear

Proverbs 9:10

The fear of the LORD is the beginning of wisdom: and the knowledge of the holy is understanding.

<u>Good Vision</u>

Looking back on days….
I see it was a blessing
But while I was yet living
It seems I just kept guessing

Were You God moving my world
So I could just keep still
But I wanted to make my own decisions
It seems out of Your Will

Whether I went right or left
I see You know the end
As a man I depended on self
Forgetting that You are my friend

Looking back on days….
Looking back on crazy nights too
I guess somebody prayed a lot
You answered like You do

Hindsight is always clear
Even though my sins are many
I realize I was living in grace
So my vision is 20/20

1 Peter 3:12

For the eyes of the Lord are over the righteous, and his ears are open unto their prayers: but the face of the Lord is against them that do evil.

Grace Time

If I only knew the date and time
that God would call me home
If I only had a glimpse of peace
to soothe the achy bone
If I knew the time I had to leave
and the sadness it would bring
If I had some sense of how it'd go
and the way the choir would sing
If I could reclaim the fleeting time
the things I had to see
If I knew the hour of my demise
would I then care less about me
If I only had another breath
and then my breath was gone
If I then but lived another day
then more love I would have shown
If I only then could change my fate
increase my time somehow
If I will the will of God's Grace for me
then I will live and love right now.

Galatians 2:20

I am crucified with Christ: nevertheless I live; yet not I, but
Christ liveth in me: and the life which I now live in the flesh
I live by the faith of the Son of God, who loved me, and gave
himself for me.

I'm Trying

We cannot stand to stand as we are; and have made ourselves
Whether dealt a foul hand or fell victim to circumstance

Instead we down each other's stance: to make up for our lack of a
stance
To somehow tear them down; to feel better about what we're
around!

Be not so full of contempt and doubt
Life's too short, not what things are about

Build up something to be your call
Everybody can't sing.....OR PLAY BALL
Don't trust in a "break" or money at all.........

Put some type of goal ahead to see
So that you can someday be what you can be!

And then be proud of the pride you found......
Stop the jealous hate and putting others down

So stop the pout and the gloom you are in...Stick out your chest
Be your own best friend

It takes only a step.........It will get hard
It is something for you.... You've got to start

Keep going slowly unto the clouds
So just look within yourself and stand there.......Proud.

Psalm 71:14

But I will hope continually, and will yet praise thee
more and more.

In Its Own Way

And worry about whether chicken or fish
While missing the hungry and those in need of a dish

And worry about whether a full choir or band
While missing the opportunity to increase God's stand

Oh Church, My Church what is your purpose to be
With all of your inward activities, no outwardly work to see

Stop the shows of fashion
Stop the praise of yourself
Stop the pedestal for people
Will a true believer be left?

Stop the let's build a building
Stop the fish that do fry
Stop the monuments to men
Will the believers just die?

I have given you a place for the whole world to see
My Church is for praising
My Church is to spread the love of me

When I then come to redeem you
My Church there to be
Have your good report in order
To then come to Me

Revelation 3:6

He that hath an ear, let him hear what the Spirit
saith unto the churches.

<u>Indictment</u>

If everybody did what I did, no movement there would be
If everyone did what I did, there would be no protest yet to see

If everybody did what I did....And only spoke their thoughts
But not speak outside of four walls
Just speak within the four walls that they bought

If everybody did what I did, slow slow change is what would be
If everyone did what I did......A lot of looking but still no see

If everybody did what I did
Watching on my butt and not from my feet
If everyone did what I did......And just observe from a soft seat

If everybody did what I did NO physical change would come to pass
If everyone did what I did.....Strong racism would just last

If everybody did what I did
And just felt bad for the hate that is done
But did not go out and with loud support
Using every excuse that is under the sun

If everybody did like I did then racism would stay the same
If everyone did like I did then the racist would keep their fame

So I challenge myself......................................
For to not have a contribution in this day
I challenge myself ....and find some "solace"
Because at least I kneeled to pray!   Give us strength Lord.
6/20/20

<u>Keep Moving</u>

You just keep pushing
Pushing
Forward to a dream
Dreaming
For something better to be seen
Seeing
Because you know there's hope within
Within
Yourself as being your own friend
Friendship
Because you can't make it all alone
Lonely
For someplace so good that you call home
Homeless
Because you haven't found the place of rest
Resting
For strength to keep pushing over quest
Quest
It would not be if pushing wasn't hard
Hard
Because you have not spoken to God
God
Jehovah, Savior, Jesus Christ
Christ
Makes all the pushing come out nice

Romans 8:28

And we know that all things work together for good to them that love God, to them who are the called according to his purpose.

<u>Keep Writing</u>

To get the gift of words and prose
And smoothness from the pen
And let the weary mind from past
Deny that thought again

If so become a lazy me
To lose the hope and win
And not to awake and start to write
Must be some type of sin!

So keep on writing
Keep on writing
The words that come from You
So keep on writing
Keep on writing
To show how I love You.

Thank You Jesus!

(L)Only Child

Seems I sit here yet today
Seems nothing wrong and no words to say
Understanding the presence and where I stay
Having my mind keep wondering yet knowing my way

No brother or sister to call my own
Even with voices not distance right on the phone
Dealing with keeping things to myself in the mental zone
But with no physical viewing still all alone

Not only myself but yet here with dad
Not singularly parented here is my mom..I'm glad
Oh what joy they bring and the fun I've had
Yet why am I wondering so and feeling so sad

My worry is few and my sadness...though mild
I don't long for many things, that's just not my style
But my emotions are whirly, unsettled for a while
I now realize my aloneness as the only child

Nevermore so sad and still happy
Just some doubt to end
I understand my reality and I feel my friend
Jesus is always with me, His Love's always been
So I just smile to myself
Cause I know I win!

So be happy for me
Inside my heart I just smile
Cause I'm in the happy place
As the only child

<u>Love Within</u>

*So sweet, so special
So dear to us and You
We share a love so great My God
A beautiful thing that is never blu*

*We thank You Precious Father
And the blessings from Above
To allow this fleshly feeling
And experience this part of love*

*And we thank You for the spiritual gifts
The love that is always true
And the lovely dust You formed for us
That all our dreams come through*

*The softness of her gentle smile
The warming eyes of glow
The moments that we get to share
The loving thoughts that flow*

*Forgive us Father, As we pause our praise
To show so great love in our life
Cause we love You God, And we love this being
Whether mother, daughter, wife*

<u>Material World</u>

Hey you're so blessed
No you're so blessed
No you're so blessed
No you are
I like the blessings from above
I like your new blue car

Yes you're so blessed
No you're so blessed
No you're so blessed
No you are
I like the blessings from above
I like your diamond star

Wow you're so blessed
No you're so blessed
No you're so blessed
No you are
I like the blessings from above
Your fame is near and far

And that be good, the bless of things
The thrill of it we see
But health and joy and peace of mind
Are blessings great for me

So bless me Lord, and bless us God
We all like things of life
And save our grace and mercy Lord
To get us out of strife

1 John 2:16

For all that is in the world, the lust of the flesh, and the lust of
the eyes and the pride of life, is not of the Father,
but is of the world.

<u>Measurement</u>

When you think of your being, and the measure you have had
And you realize the measure of true worth
And its being is glad

The measure is nothing but a ruler of the man
But God's units are amounts you can't
…..Measure with your hand

Not an inch or a foot or a yard or a pound
Can measure your strength
When the Holy Spirit is found

In the measure of God, not the unit of men
You can't hold the power
Of your inner true Friend

The change is coming
The change is coming
The measure is new
Man can only be measured
With the Spirit God puts in you

Matthew 7:2

For with what judgment ye judge, ye shall be judged: and with
What measure you mete, it shall be measured to you again.

<u>Messenger</u>

Why would You make my road so bumpy
If Your People need Your Words

Why would You stand the critics up so strong
Reviewing what was heard

Why would You cause a slight adjustment
In my health or in my plans
What is the reason You are pulling
From the stability of the man

Why would You cause or allow such pain to rise
From others that bear Your Name
What is the purpose for the struggle
Or is it the testing just the same

Reveal Your reason or Your Purpose
So this man can continue to grow
Show Your Holy Wisdom now Lord
Your child has urgent need to know

BLESS ME WITH YOUR MERCY LORD

2 Timothy 4:2

Preach the word; be instant in season, out of season; reprove, rebuke, exhort with all long suffering and doctrine.

<u>Modern Living</u>

We are all different in how......
We see and we seek
The face of God is the same
Yet each walk is unique

Is the hearing all level
While an ear is in place
Is the seeing the same
Or just two spots on the face

When you play the life game
Don't be righteous fools
The game can be played different
But still follows the same rules

Can the mouth open and close
In and out as things go
How is the mind wired so simple
But complex thoughts there to know

Is it so difficult and yet easy
Still one thing keeps Its Name
Everyone may think themselves different
But the Holy Word stays the same

New Man

I'm here a score and plus a five
I must now be a man
Yet on my mother and on my dad
On them I still do stand

With arms and chest I spread and grow
With hair upon my face
I am a man I'm all grown up
But don't have my own place

I play the part I've grown so smart
I know the things of street
I've loved them all I am a man
I've left lives on the sheets

I stand and pause and look around
I rule what I survey
I am a man I am a king
I don't care what you say

And then at night or early morn
"Did mom bake cookies chunk"
I need a snack I am a man
...............But truly just a punk

<u>No Doubt</u>

Not one minute go down your mental road of regret
For God's Wisdom guides your life
And in this moment.......His Will is met

And your choice to agree or somehow take blame
With unfulfillment in His Will.......
Keeps your mind in the same

Your latter is better than you can ever see
And giving in finally to His Will.......
Will leave you better than be

For the soul is alive and its purpose is clear
But you have to inspect closely
To see and to hear

Not just looking with sight or just hearing with sound
For in scripture and prayer
True purpose is found

Yet live now in the present and learn from the past
The life you live will be your measure
Teaching your spirit to last

<u>No Sting</u>

The sun comes around soon
The moon comes around soon
The life of man is as bright as the sun
And ends like the settling of the moon

Over the last eight days
There were four funerals of I knew
They all were aware of You God
And the homegoings referenced to You too

Death is too........Part of life
Seems for the living we cry
For a blessing came out of this moment
Holy Spirit please catch us when we die

In the grip of the sadness
And as the water swells the eye
Tears will just comfort the living
Dealing with such emotion......we try

The stillness does take a toll
In the stillness we do yet toil
Still like the Good Book keeps reading
We must all return to the soil

1 Thessalonians 4:14

For if we believe that Jesus died and rose again, even so them also which sleep in Jesus will God bring with him.

<u>OK Me</u>

How can I justify my guilt
When it is only known within
Is not my cause to not obey
Is it just simply called a sin

A sin is strong a sin is wicked
And I am surely none of that
The things that make you sinful show
Your self is vile just like a rat

So what I do or what I did
Will not condemn my entire soul
I'm only guilty of just living
No one's an angel to behold

So if you think like me don't worry
We will all just be OK
'Cause my sins like yours aren't too deadly
They were just wrong part of the day

Just wait on God, you know to pray
He is there for you to tell
But don't be foolish change right now
So you won't be talking up from hell

1 Corinthians 4:5

Therefore judge nothing before the time, until the Lord come, who both will bring to light the hidden things of darkness, and will make manifest the counsels of the hearts: and then shall every man have praise of God.

Pick Sides

In this life as it is going
In this world that we see
In this question of a spirit
Opposite sides yet seem to be

The actions and the moments
To the ying and the yang
The truth and yet a lie....exists
To the balance life just hangs

In a world that's parallel
In a good contradicts a bad
In a strong show of human pride
Only the Holy Spirit ends up sad

Caught up in sin and yet living
The darkest thoughts get some light
The things that once seemed in the closet
Are out in day and out in night

Just keep doing what you want
Just keep doing the man thing
Just keep letting flesh lead you
Just keep not hearing angels sing

The world is shaky and it's sliding
The man has let his ego swell
The world in shame...yet not hiding!
Side with Heaven or slide to hell

Romans 7:25

I thank God through Jesus Christ our Lord. So then with the
mind I myself serve the law of God;
but with the flesh the law of sin.

PSSSST

Always expecting God to do the extraordinary
Damn near raising the dead
When we do less than ordinary
On Sunday, we just stay in the bed

Always with a thought of what we pray for
And the simple things we can get
Thank God He doesn't have our commitment
Or on our blessings He'd just quit

With our sins so nasty and bad
Just makes God want to spit
Sin so bad it can't be used as fertilizer
Eventhough it smells like some.....

So fed up with the hypocrisy
The world only revolves around me
With these selfish thoughts of only self
What else could God really see

So here we are at an impasse
Should God let us live or just die
I hope His Decision stays in grace
And God with His Mercy lets us by

Getting by means having some more time
To get our sinful stuff together
We've been warned with sickness, death and pain
Now the last warning...is in the weather

Revelation 16:1

And I heard a great voice out of the temple saying to the seven
angels, Go your ways, and pour out the vials
of the wrath of God upon the Earth.

<u>Seems Like</u>

It seems the ground should be wet
But God let it be dry
It seems that I would not make it
But God let me get by

It seems the ground should be dry
But God let it be wet
It seems in my strength I could win
But alone I still lost that bet

It seems when I see with my eyes
God just wants me to hear
It seems when I think there's no hope
God just draws me more near

It seems when I hear with my ears
God just wants me to see
It seems that when I'm walking alone
God is just there guiding me

It seems an impossible feat
For my soul that God gave
Seems like God gave up a lot
For my soul to be saved

It seems like God did it again
Seems there's more joy to be gained
God is still over all
I'm too in awe to explain

It is an impossible feat
Seems like God did it again
When I knew I would lose
I ended up.....with a win

Psalm 31:24

Be of good courage, and he shall strengthen your heart,
all ye that hope in the LORD.

<u>Six Sign</u>

Riding in on six white horses
Now you want to do some more sin
Fussing, Cussing, cattle rustling
Just can't trust in a friend

Yes it's frightening and true like lightening
As the sound rushes in
Yes it's false the air is tossing
With "7" miles blowing wind

See the Thunder hear the flashes
Still don't know where you've been
Life is flipping time is slipping
Thinking what will be then

Apocalyptic…yet it's scripted
If you think it's the end
Take comfort saints it's not a prank
You know still…we will win

All the speeches talk that teaches
Fogs a mind mired in
"The Revelation" gives a clue
Why not read it again

When you don't know then you don't know
Yet you're strong as some tin
Get the mark and keep on looking
Just don't blink in the end

Revelation 14:11

And the smoke of their torment ascendeth up for ever and ever: and they have no rest day nor night, who worship the beast and his image, and whosoever receiveth the mark of his name

<u>Still Seems Like</u>

Seems like I wasn't gonna make it
Seems like I struggle all day
Seems like when I started to give up
Seems like the Holy Spirit urged me to pray

Seems like the devil is at me
Seems like he is right on my heel
Seems like he is bothering my health
Seems like he is increasing my bills

Seems like I'm almost at end
Seems like I won't ever win
Seems like I know I'm alone
Even though it seems I have lots of friends

Seems like the day will be dreary
But God......I need the sunshine
Seems like I need to keep looking
Seems there's some peace I can find

Job 11:18

You will be secure, because there is hope; you will look
about you and take your rest in safety

<u>**Stranger Prayer**</u>

Pray for me, please pray for me
I know I'm not a stranger
Please pray for me, pray for me
You know my soul's in danger

Pray for me like you pray for them
Because they are in pain
Pray for me, please pray for me
Like victims in the rain

Pray for me like the unknown name
That is on the prayer list
Pray for me like you pray for them
That cancer just did miss

With sincerity and lovingness
For the unknown yet pray to God
But with intimate knowledge of
And yet so hard to start

How easy to the prayer for those
That never have been met
But difficult the prayer for me
And next to you I'm set

James 5:16

Therefore confess your sins to each other and
pray for each other so that you may be healed. The prayer of a
righteous person is powerful and effective.

Straw Vote

To things that have become aware
And life is so unfairing
The truth of life the circumstance
Leaves thoughts of no one caring

But to the man the wonderful man
The man that runs to mischief
Be unaware and unassume
The times and things that's shifted

To change a color on a face
To side with what seems mild
And realize that the choice is made
With thoughts unlike a child

A strange embrace but still embrace
Alignment of the times
And unassume, and farther from
A goal we still can't find

God is in control He is in control!
And whatever He allows
And even though we are unaware
He still makes to whom we bow

<u>Study On</u>

How does it feel to have Christian friends
That seem to secretly hope you fail

How do you say stay on your own way
And don't walk straight into hell

How do you feel the faith and love
That is needed to then succeed
And get enough from the dust
To help grow the little seeds

How can a man claim so great glory
Yet contribute none to man
And with that pride unto himself
And even attempt to count the sand

How does the wolf dressed up as sheep
But true lambs are never led astray
And sin that bites with fangs of evil
Do the slaughter day to day

Only clearance of repentance, and forgiving
And not pay
Unbind the letters of the Book
Free the Spirit on today

Romans 8:36

As it is written, For thy sake we are killed all the day long; we are accounted as sheep for the slaughter.

<u>Teen Change</u>

Hey, Hey....Please hear the words I tell you
Or just ignore the Word that's said
You keep on living how you want
Then all you'll do is end up dead

You just keep bobbing all around
Not knowing the damages that you've done
You just crushed the Holy Spirit
All in the name of having fun

You have just shamed all your people
By following some spirit that is lead....
You straight to a realm of total darknesss
Look in the mirror at your head

Us Christians know you call us names
Thinking we don't like the way you dance
Now we think your movements are kinda cool
But please just pull up on your pants

It makes no mindful common sense
To align your look with simple thugs
Did you get dropped on your head
Or did you just not get enough hugs

Please stop to take a look or pause
Your life is heading for a doom
Ask God for help, talk to your people
Then go clean up on your room

The Blood

As the Blood flows up
From my ankle to my knee
Let it flow back to my feet
So I step where I need to be

As the flowing goes around
Through my body to my heart
Let it give strength to my spirit
So I always make good starts

Around me fully into my arm
Let the blood flow to my brain
Back to my hand and to my arm
To help shelter me from pain

Let Your Blood be a filter
For all the things I see
As It flows into my joints
As It runs back through my knees

Filter hearing, Filter speech
Filter touching, Filter sound
Let the Blood within me flow
Keep It moving all around

The life and strength, the importance
The symbol of blood flowing from my head
Reflects the love You have for me
Through the Blood that Jesus shed

And as the Blood remains contained
In the Spirit that You mold
Keep It filtered by Your Wisdom
So my blood saves my soul

1 John 1:7

But if we walk in the light, as he is in the light, we have
fellowship one with another, and the blood of Jesus Christ his
Son cleanseth us from all sin.

The Holy Word

The hand placed on a strange square box
Some words there seemed to say
But fingers, palm, and shadows hide
The words from view this day

What could it be appears a book
Some antique thing of old
With leather bound and neatly trimmed
With inlaid things of gold

It is a book and what's a book
A thing with canvas ink
And no one reads or knows the words
Or even seems to think

The inner being of this thing
Conveys a moral life
Like do not kill and do not steal
And marry man to wife

And there it is two sacred words
One is B.I.B.L.E
And the other word from all acclaim
Just for the world to see

And just like that the moment passed
An official promise for both
And on a Book that no one reads
Confirms a legal oath

John 1:1

In the beginning was the Word, and the Word was with God,
and the Word was God.

<u>They Who</u>

They tell me "don't you fall"
While evil is all around me
They say "overcome temptation"
But evil's four walls still stall me

They tell me "not to go"
But staying here don't make me strong
They say "you'll find escape"
But just being here seems wrong

They tell me to "fight the fight"
While punching air is hard for me
They tell me to "fight within"
But I can't fight spirits I don't see

They tell me "you can win"
While every time I seem to lose
They tell me "pray the more"
But leaning on hope I must refuse

They tell me "you'll get healing"
While every day is still a grind
They tell me "we" are praying
But more faith I need to find

They tell me all of this and that
But I say tell me stuff no more
They say "keep talking to Jesus"
I'll just have some questions.....at heaven's door

Hebrews 11:1

Now faith is the substance of things hoped for,
the evidence of things not seen.

<u>Think Again</u>

What if you thought you were getting closer to God
But God thought you were beginning to fail
What if you thought you were heading toward heaven
But God thought you were closer to hell

What if you thought you were being righteous
And the great insights you have learned
But all the angels looked on sadly
They saw you a future of slow burn

What if you carried your Holy Bible
But never read all of the words
And you stood strong at church each week
But preaching is something you just heard

What if you smiled because you knew fact
That the Lord was definitely your friend
But truly your soul had not changed
And you were nearing a bad end

What if you listed all your Godly work
And all church activities you were in
What if you called on Jesus loudly
But your soul was still stuck in sin

What if this realization happened
In a fairly decent range....
Would you then take heed quickly
So your heart could make that change

Acts 17:30

And the times of this ignorance God winked at; but now commandeth all men every where to repent:

<u>What Did You</u>

Did you just leave...there stands a dash
And now you're gone
Did you leave nothing behind
Except the loved alone

Did you even feel or note
Some others' pain and strife
Did you just move and slide along
And keep to your own life

Did you watch the news, shed a tear
For those in cold and rain
Did you just shrug and shake your head
And do for your own gain

Did you think to share a pleasing word
Some life to stop from down
Did you just say it's tough today
Then close your eyes to sound

Did you live your life to fill the dash
From birth now unto death
Did you mark your dash a prideful check
To promote only self

Did you succeed with your own things
And execute your skillful plan
Did you just breathe a mindless life
Not being a Godfilled man

Did you listen well but not learn
Just not hear the Word said
Did you just keep to keep too late
Now find yourself dead

Mark 8:38

Whosoever therefore shall be ashamed
of me and of my words in this adulterous and sinful generation;
of him also shall the Son of man be ashamed when
he comes in the glory of his Father with the holy angels.

<u>What Job</u>

The Holy Spirit came to me and gave me a great task
I wondered what the task would be
And how long the task would last

The Spirit said I'll show you all
How great of great this task
And soon to know and fulfill all
Starts only when you ask

So ask is what I'll do today
To start a task to keep
I'll ask a great question of life
And do it before I sleep

My question is how long it lasts
This sinning of the saints
This forgetting of Commandments Ten
The holy thoughts that seem so faint

How long it lasts the pain of wrong
The who of Jesus Christ
And sin and sin and sin and sin
So called Christians seem un..nice

My task must be to open eyes
To maybe shed some light
The reply was quick and simple too
I was told "continue to write"

Habakkuk 2:2

And the LORD answered me, and said, Write the vision, and make it plain upon tables, that he may run that readeth it.

<u>What Spirit</u>

With water rushing to an unyielding boil
Not responding or considering a worker's true toil
Heaped on by criticism and contradictions
With unreflection as foil
Stress related pressure rises and doesn't cease
Until you're under soil

Through the existence like a river
A tributary to the sea
As the Holy Spirit claims a grip
The naysayers rise to be

And yet withholding the flood's true power
Keep remaining within the bounds of land
As the face of God is sought
But a droplet is still held by Satan's hand

Only a tiny change of matter
Effects the total body lake
Filter cleansing peaceful water
As you're flowing for Christ's sake

Watch Over Me Lord

What the .....

Is it all almost over
Is it coming to an end
Are we where events are proving true
And exposing endless sin

Hey Satan is on the TV
Being portrayed by a handsome man
And he talks about his power
And how he rules this sinful land

There are murders and mass killings
And some tricking and some cheating
Even the sin is on the ground
Or is the judgement in what we're eating

The earth revolving, history rolling
Noise so loud you have no sound
Sinful spirits rewrite knowledge
Speaking this place is flat, not round

The Good Book says it's going to happen
And the Word says happen quick
With no healing the world around us
Just brings death from being sick

Don't change your ways keep sinning
And then sin the more and more
Your path leads past heaven's window
Right straight into hell's open door

Isaiah 59:7

Their feet run to evil, and they make haste to shed innocent blood: their thoughts are thoughts of iniquity; wasting and destruction are in their paths.

<u>You Thinking</u>

And you call yourself a Christian
And you say that Jesus is a friend
Going on about your worship
Ignoring all Commandments 10

Yet you call yourself a Christian
And you love your fellow man
Making sure you get all first
No thought of giving helping hands

Yet you state that you're a Christian
And you live in all God's Grace
Haven't been to church or prayed much
But you plan to see His Face

And yet you judge all that's not Christian
'Cause you call yourself a saint
Do you think that makes a Christian
Have all your senses just gone faint

And you call yourself a Christian
Yet the things you do and say
Deny the name of Jesus Christ
Hurting God on everyday

2 Chronicles 7:14

If my people, which are called by my name, shall humble themselves, and pray, and seek my face, and turn from their wicked ways; then will I hear from heaven, and will forgive their sin, and will heal their land.

<u>Your Will</u>

Lord help my mind and keep me still
Please open my heart to hear Your Will

Lord steady my walk for Your Light to show
Keep planting Your Spirit for Your Will to grow

I know for me Your Son was killed
Please put me on the path
To Your Will fulfill

Instill in me the more and more
Your Will to overcome sin
Like I did before

Lord stengthen me strong
To resist the fleshly thrill
Help me to walk into the Kingdom
And stay in....Your Will

1 Peter 2:11

Dearly beloved, I beseech you as strangers and pilgrims, abstain fleshly lusts, which war against the soul.

Living with Divine Intervention
Inspiring phrases to enlighten your walk with God; fresh
thoughts to help lift your burdens and challenge you to get closer
to the Word. And by doing so, get closer to our Lord and Savior,
Jesus Christ!

B. Chuck Thomas
"TheOldPoetHimself"